Labor Day

By Carmen Bredeson

Consultants
Nanci R. Vargus, Ed.D.
Primary Multiage Teacher
Decatur Township Schools, Indianapolis, Indiana

Katharine A. Kane, Reading Specialist
Former Language Arts Coordinator,
San Diego County Office of Education

Children's Press®
A Division of Scholastic Inc.
New York   Toronto   London   Auckland   Sydney
Mexico City   New Delhi   Hong Kong
Danbury, Connecticut

Designer: Herman Adler Design
Photo Researcher: Caroline Anderson
The photo on the cover shows the Labor Day Parade in New York City.

Library of Congress Cataloging-in-Publication Data

Bredeson, Carmen.
    Labor Day / by Carmen Bredeson.
        p. cm. — (Rookie read-about holidays)
    Includes index.
    Summary: The history, meaning, and customs of Labor Day are
presented in this introductory book.
        ISBN 0-516-22378-X (lib. bdg.)   0-516-26312-9 (pbk.)
    1. Labor Day—Juvenile literature. 2. Labor unions—Juvenile literature.
[1. Labor Day. 2. Labor unions. 3. Holidays.] I. Title. II. Series.
HD7791 .B74   2001
394.264—dc21
                                                                00-047567

Pack the picnic basket
and strike up the band.
It's Labor Day!

Labor Day is a holiday in the United States. People celebrate it on the first Monday in September.

Labor Day marks the end of the summer.

September 2001

Sunday	Monday	Tuesday	Wednesday	Thursday	Friday	Saturday
						1
2	3	4	5	6	7	8
9	10	11	12	13	14	15
16	17	18	19	20	21	22
23/30	24	25	26	27	28	29

Labor is another word for work. We honor American workers on Labor Day.

People get a day off from their jobs. Many towns have picnics and parades.

Different kinds of workers march in Labor Day parades.

Some are firefighters, teachers, and factory workers.

Factories are places full
of big machines. These
machines make things, such
as toys, computers, and cars.

The first factories made
tractors, wagons, and cloth.

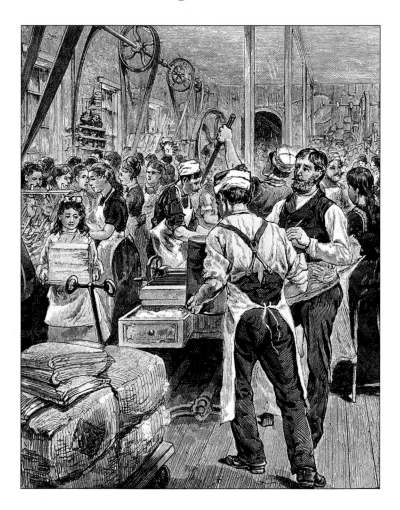

Long ago, many factories were dirty and dangerous.

The air was full of smoke and dust.

Workers often got hurt using the big machines.

People spent twelve hours
a day at their jobs.

Poor children worked, too.
They did not go to school.

Some people complained about their jobs. But factory owners did not always listen.

17

A union meeting

The workers wanted
to make things better.
They started groups
called labor unions.

A group has more power
than just one person.
Factory owners paid
attention to the unions.

If an owner did not listen,
the union called a strike.
Nobody in the union went
to work during a strike.

The factory shut down,
and the owner lost money.

21

Workers did not come back until the owners made the factories better.

The owners cleaned up the buildings. They made the workdays shorter.

The government also passed laws.

Factories had to be safe for the workers. It became a crime for children to work there.

Today, unions are not just for factory workers. There are unions for teachers, builders, actors, and others.

Labor Day helps us remember how things have changed.

Let's give a big cheer for American workers!

29

Words You Know

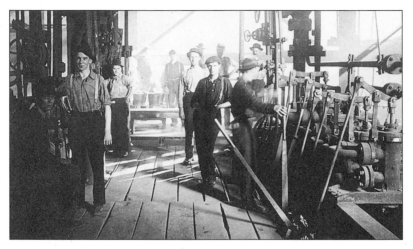

factory

labor union

machines

parade

picnic

strike

Index

About the Author

Carmen Bredeson is the author of twenty-five books for children. She lives in Texas and enjoys doing research and traveling.

Photo Credits

Photographs ©: Archive Photos: 13, 30 top; Corbis-Bettmann: 8 (George Hall), 10, 31 top left (David Lees), 17, 18; North Wind Picture Archives: 11, 21, 31 bottom right; PhotoEdit: 26, 30 bottom (Robert Brenner), 7, 29, 31 top right (Gary A. Conner), 9 (Spencer Grant), 6, 31 bottom left (Michael Newman), cover (Rudi Von Briel), 25 (D. Young-Wolff); Superstock, Inc.: 14 (Lewis Hine), 3, 22.